SKY HIGH
SUSSEX COAST

PHOTOGRAPHY BY JASON HAWKES

First published in Great Britain in 2009

Photographs © 2009 Jason Hawkes

British Library Cataloguing-in-Publication Data
A CIP record for this title is available from the British Library

ISBN 978 1 906887 56 8

PiXZ Books
Halsgrove House, Ryelands Industrial Estate,
Bagley Road, Wellington, Somerset TA21 9PZ
Tel: 01823 653777
Fax: 01823 216796
email: sales@halsgrove.com

An imprint of Halstar Ltd, part of the Halsgrove group of companies
Information on all Halsgrove titles is available at: www.halsgrove.com

Printed and bound by Grafiche Flaminia, Italy

Introduction

The Sussex coast stretches eastwards from Hampshire some 90 miles (145km) from Thorney Island within Chichester Harbour to the Kent boundary near Camber Sands. Interspersed with its major coastal towns and small villages lies some of the finest scenery in Southern England, including the magnificent white chalk cliffs of Beachy Head and the Seven Sisters.

The photographs in this book cover the whole coast, between Selsey Bill and Beachy Head, and then from Beachy Head to Dungeness (over the border in Kent). Also included is the conurbation of Brighton, Hove, Worthing and Littlehampton. It has a population of over 450,000, and stretches for some 30 miles (50km) from Littlehampton in the west to Seaford in the east. Other major settlements on the coastline are Chichester, Bognor Regis, Eastbourne and Hastings.

Jason Hawkes is one of the country's best-known photographers specialising in aerial photography. The photographs in this book are selected to provide the reader with an overview of a variety of landscapes and settlements, with historic sites included. *Sky High Sussex Coast* is a perfect memento of this historic coast.

Near West Itchenor, Chichester Harbour.

Right: Low water Chichester Harbour.

East Wittering.

Left: West Wittering lies at the eastern mouth of Chichester Harbour.

Funfair at West Sands, east of Selsey.

Right: Selsey, at the southernmost tip of the Manhood Peninsula, derives its name from 'Seal Island'.

Once a thriving port, and home of smugglers, Pagham Harbour is now a nature reserve. Pagham Lagoon, seen centre, used to be the outlet to Pagham Harbour in the late 1800s.

Overleaf: A truly stunning view inland over Pagham.

Aldwick, now part of the built-up area west of Bognor Regis.

Right: Bognor Regis.

The Butlins resort at Bognor Regis.

Right: Bognor's neighbour, Felpham.

Littlehampton nestles at the foot of the South Downs, at the mouth of the River Arun.

Grand Avenue, Worthing.

Left: Looking down on to Marine Crescent, Worthing.

Marine Parade, Worthing.

Worthing Pier.

A superb view over Worthing, with Lancing and Shoreham beyond.

South Lancing, with the Sussex Downs beyond.

Left: Looking west over Worthing.

Northwards over Lancing and Sompting.

Right: Shoreham-by-the-Sea.

Hove seafront, King's Esplanade.

Left: Shoreham Harbour.

A panoramic view of Hove.

Right: Where Hove meets Brighton, and the ruins of the old pier.

The funfair at the end of Brighton pier.

Left: Brighton pier.

Waterloo Street and Norfolk Square, Brighton.

Right: Saltdean, its famous Lido visible mid foreground.

The view east along the shore from Saltdean, and onwards to Peacehaven and Beachy Head.

Newhaven looking along 'The Cut'. The fort, on the headland (left), was built around the 1860s.

Left: Towards Seaford Bay and Newhaven.

Cuckmere Haven.

Left: Seaford.

The famous Seven Sisters chalk cliffs, looking towards Cuckmere Haven.

Right: Beachy Head and the Seven Sisters.

Eastbourne pier.

Left: The eastward view over Eastbourne.

Grand Hotel, Eastbourne.

The College Road area, Eastbourne.

Eastbourne's Wish Tower.

Above Howard Square, Eastbourne.

Eastbourne Harbour.

The marina, Eastbourne.

The Martello Tower, Pevensey Bay, now converted into a residence.

Right: The coast between Pevensey and Bexhill.

West of Bexhill.

Bexhill-on-Sea.

West Parade, Bexhill.

Right: Bexhill overlooking De La Warr Parade.

Bulverhythe, between Bexhill and St Leonard's-on-Sea.

Hastings.

East of Hastings, Cliff End.

Right: Winchelsea.

Low tide, Rye Bay.